Fugitive/Refuge

Also by Philip Metres

Fugitive/Refuge

Philip Metres

COPPER CANYON PRESS

PORT TOWNSEND, WASHINGTON

Front cover: Chiharu Shiota, *The Key in the Hand,* 2015.
Installation: old keys, wooden boats, red wool.
Japan Pavilion at 56th Venice Biennale,
Venice, Italy. Photo by Sunhi Mang.
© 2023 Artists Rights Society (ARS),
New York / VG Bild-Kunst, Bonn, and the artist.

Inside covers: Chiharu Shiota, *Tracing Boundaries,* 2021.
Installation: wool, metal frame, door. EMMA – Espoo Museum of Modern
Art, Espoo, Finland. Photo by Paula Virta / EMMA – Espoo
Museum of Modern Art. Courtesy of Saastamoinen
Foundation / EMMA – Espoo Museum of Modern Art.
© 2023 Artists Rights Society (ARS), New York / VG
Bild-Kunst, Bonn, and the artist.

Copper Canyon Press is in residence at Fort Worden State Park in Port Townsend,
Washington, under the auspices of Centrum. Centrum is a gathering place for artists
and creative thinkers from around the world, students of all ages and backgrounds, and
audiences seeking extraordinary cultural enrichment.

LIBRARY OF CONGRESS CATALOGING-IN-PUBLICATION DATA
Names: Metres, Philip, 1970– author.
Title: Fugitive/refuge / Philip Metres.
Description: Port Townsend, Washington : Copper Canyon Press, 2024. |
Summary: "A collection of poems by Philip Metres"— Provided by publisher.
Identifiers: LCCN 2023042477 (print) | LCCN 2023042478 (ebook) |
ISBN 9781556596698 (paperback) | ISBN 9781619322929 (epub)
Subjects: LCGFT: Poetry.
Classification: LCC PS3613.E887 F84 2024 (print) |
LCC PS3613.E887 (ebook) | DDC 811/.6—dc23/eng/20231012
LC record available at https://lccn.loc.gov/2023042477
LC ebook record available at https://lccn.loc.gov/2023042478

9 8 7 6 5 4 3 2 FIRST PRINTING

COPPER CANYON PRESS
Post Office Box 271
Port Townsend, Washington 98368
www.coppercanyonpress.org

Acknowledgments

Thanks to the ancestors, who made their way and in whose wake we walk each day.

Thanks to the following, where these poems have appeared:

The Academy of American Poets Poem-a-Day, *America, American Poetry Journal, The American Poetry Review, Asheville Poetry Review, The Believer, Bellingham Review, Broadsided Press, Cordite Poetry Review, DIAGRAM, Diode, Fjords Review, Image, Inverted Syntax, Jewish Currents, jubilat, The Kenyon Review, Mizna, Narrative, New England Review, On the Seawall, POEM, Poetry, Poetry International, River Styx, Rumpus, Rusted Radishes, Seneca Review, Southern Indiana Review, Tin House, Under a Warm Green Linden.*

The Book of Scented Things: 100 Contemporary Poems about Perfume (Literary House Press), *February: An Anthology* (February Press), *Voices on the Move: An Anthology by and about Refugees* (Solis Press).

Thanks to Elizabeth Bradfield and Broadsided Press for publishing a broadside of "The Trees in My Chest," in collaboration with artist Sara Tabbert, and including it in their anthology.

Thanks to Lisa Neher for collaborating on a musical composition called "When My Daughter Asked Why There Are Stars, I Said," based on the poem *"Why are there stars?"*

Thanks to the Akron Art Museum for commissioning "Night, Come Tenderly, Hold Us" which appeared in a postcard series of poems responding to works of art at the museum.

Thanks to Amy Breau, Jessica Cuello, Ilya Kaminsky, Christopher Kempf, Dave Lucas, E.J. McAdams, Tomás Q. Morín, and Mary Weems, for their helpful comments on the poems and on versions of this book.

Thanks to the John Simon Guggenheim Memorial Foundation, John Carroll University, Lannan Foundation, and the Ohio Arts Council, for providing support during the writing of this book.

Thanks to Michael Wiegers, Ashley E. Wynter, Claretta Holsey, Ryo Yamaguchi, Marie Landau, Phil Kovacevich, David Caligiuri, Rowan Sharp, and Copper Canyon Press for believing in this book and bringing it into being.

And first and last, Alpha and Omega, to all the names of the Unnameable, all praise.

for the ancestors

أهلا و سهلا

Welcome.

You're among family.

The way is easy. Open.

Contents

Border/Manifest II

II. رحيل (Of Exile)

Border/Manifest III

III. فخر (Of Return)

Fugitive/Refuge

قَصِيدَة

In the *Book of Poetry and Poets* (ninth century), Ibn Qutaybah outlines the conventions of the qasidah, an Arabic poetic form in three parts:

In the nasīb, which means "fate," the poet is in a nostalgic mood. Sometimes, pursuing the beloved, the poet will come upon the remains of a camp, the beloved's caravan, causing a consideration of what has passed.

In the rahīl, the poet travels outside of the known, outside the tribe, facing the cruelty of the world.

The final section, in which the poet makes a return of sorts, may assume a number of genres: the fakhr, praise of the tribe; the madīh, praise of the tribe's leader; the hijā', which satirizes enemies; the hikma, which offers moral precepts.

Qasida for the End of Time

I. PLAGUE PSALM 40

I wait in the waiting room
Of my room for you, dear doctor,

To lean down and listen to
The weird music in my chest.

Draw me out of the mire
Of terminal detention,

Renewable distress.
I'm surrounded, suffocated

Inside a gated state.
The wind scribbles invitations

Only tethered branches answer.
Maestro, steady my starlings.

For you I hunger. Lift your baton
And stuff my mouth with singing.

Once, salt was the power to cross the unmapped
and sidle up to the one hauling the story

of why the caravan was moving, and where. Once
story was a song that mapped the rising horizon

and water the reason to pitch houses of hair or hide
or load everything on shoulders. Once alone

was shieldlessness, prelude to danger. Once God
was mountain thunder, or drought, or floods,

something to sacrifice a child to, the fist of justice
slowly opening. Then God was a flaming shrub, then

a tickle in your insomniac ear. Once forgetfulness
was waking hungover, alarmed, driving to a dying

factory in a Rust Belt town. Then it was running
past empty in the middle of winter, testing the limits

of emptiness. Once there were highway robbers. Then
freeways with toll plazas, oases of hamburgers, temples

of the mavens of convenience. Once perpetuity
was an aquiline profile hewn from marble or stone.

Then a map of everything you named yourself
after yourself. Then it was writing your name

in cold Pacific iambic. Then a yacht, a kilo of blow,
bikini stock options. And now it's becoming

one's own constellation, dim planets basking
in your digital light. Once bridges were ice roads,

and the bride of the sea was the name of a city.
Once a wall was meant to slow invaders. Now

deserts move faster than future, but still can't catch
up to history. In twilight, across a Managua freeway,

sweatshop workers flow, then skitter across
asphalt lanes toward dirt-floor villages, their white tees

gleaming in headlights like doe eyes. Once existence
was hand to mouth. Then it was stone oven. Then

nostalgia for hunger, weight watching. Then watching
through rearview mirror a whole forest dress up

in smoke and flame. Once you could drive, not knowing
where you were going. Then you couldn't drive

without your phone telling you where. Once the car
began to shake so hard we thought it was laughing.

Then we thought it was dying, and we were
going to die. All it needed was tires. Once feet were

tires. Once hands were wipers, cupholders, car seats,
horns. Once scarves were windshields, veils for eyes

reflecting the road ahead and the road they rode
to arrive in the middle of things, not wondering about the end.

3. AT THE ARAB AMERICAN WEDDING

great-uncles in tuxes played gin,
        drank scotch, counted

        cash by the pool
like extras from *The Godfather.*

Inside, aunts had long given up
        the old country—

        or else wrapped it,
carefully, inside grape leaves.

The black already canonical:
        fedoras & hair,

        olives & eyes—
stories lilting like ash at the end

of smokes. In ballroom haze we danced
        dabke—clasped hands

        with cousins we knew
or barely knew, arms braiding arms,

feet stepping as if into dark,
        lifting & dragged

        back & forth,
as if the foot were snagged

on a fit of remembering—
        facing each other

        we faced each other
& circled some invisible

tree our dancing made—limbs reaching—
          no longer speaking

          the tongue we once
held common, we grasp for branches

to keep this circle moving, forth
          & back, forth & back—

          stamping ourselves
into a land so far from homeland.

Border/Manifest I

Unframed by any photograph, diminished by history,
rehearsed in no song,
embalmed by oral memory, great-grandfather
where have you gone?

"The Ballad of Skandar"

Dramatis Personae

Iskandar (Skandar) ibn Mitri Abourjaili	great-grandfather, died 1923
Elena Abourjaili/Metres	great-grandmother, 1887–1935
Felipe (also Philip) Metres	grandfather, 1907–1993
Philip Metres Jr.	father, 1942–present
Philip Metres III	self, 1970–present
Naguib/Najeeb (also Miguel, Jim) Metres	great-uncle, 1900–1977
Teresa Metres	great-aunt, 1908–1982
Adell Metres Nahom	great-aunt, 1906–2002
Helen Nahom	great-aunt, Adell's daughter, 1933–present
Salomon Metriz, also Sam Metres	great-uncle, 1910–1990
Alexander (also Mitri) Metres	great-uncle, 1920–1937

man·i·fest (i)

\ˈma-nə-ˌfest\

from the Latin manus *(hand)* + festus *(able to be seized or grasped)*

    1. clear or obvious to the eye or mind

As in *The system's manifest failings*

Antonym:
secret

    2. be evidence of; prove

As in *Civil unrest is often manifested in robberies and murder*

Antonym:
mask

    3. (of an ailment) become apparent through the appearance of symptoms

As in *A disorder that usually manifests in middle age*

Antonym:
hide

    4. (of a ghost or spirit) appear

As in *After he was killed, he manifested in the form of a bird*

أغنية اسكندر [1] (The Ballad of Skandar II)

دير القمر، لبنان[2]

لم يتأطّر في أي صورة، أنقصه [3]
التاريح،
لم تجر عليه تدريبات في أغنية،
حُنِّط بذاكرة شفهية/ يا أيّها الجد الأكبر
إلى أين ذهبت؟ [4]

تحت القمر المنحسر، في وادي
دير القمر
اسكندر بن ميتري ——— عربي،
مسيحي، من جنود المحتلّ.

---

1 See "The Ballad of Skandar," *To See the Earth* (Cleveland State University Poetry Center, 2008). Arabic translation by Samuel Shimon, for *Banipal* (2014).

2 The village of Deir al-Qamar is in the Shouf mountain region of Lebanon. Its name means "Monastery of the Moon." According to local lore, the Druze amir had ordered his soldiers to dig into the rocky earth. If they found an Islamic symbol, they were to build a mosque. If they found a Christian one, a church. They stabbed the stony land until their muscles ached and their spades were dull. A man called out, waving the others over. On an uncovered rock, they could make out both a cross and a moon.

3 When I return to Deir al-Qamar in 2019, I see in the distant mountains the gleam of snow. Lebanon, it's said, derives from the word meaning "white," because of its snowy peaks.

4 "Once upon a time," in Arabic fairy tales, translates as "there was and there was not." Maybe it happened, maybe it didn't. There was and there was not, in the moon's monastery, a boy born. They named him Iskandar ibn Mitri Abourjaili.

في أقصى أطراف الامبراطورية العثمانية،⁵
فوق بلدة صغيرة،
غيّر مسلمٌ مجرى الحياة،
تتداول القصة،

لتروي المحاصيل. المسيحيون في الأسفل⁶
أرسلوا جنديا وراء جنديا.
لم يستطيعوا القبض على عديم الاسم⁷
المسلم المكّار. إلى أن أحضر⁸

---

5   Iskandar ibn Mitri Abourjaili translates as Alexander, son of Mitri Abourjaili. Alexander means "defender of men." Abourjaili translates as "father of men." According to family history, in the seventeenth century, after our ancestor Atallah's sons showed courage in their defense of Beirut, the amir bestowed the last name as an honorific.

     a   One could translate, if one is a literalist, Iskandar's full name as Defender of Men of the Father of Men. Warrior of Warriors. I'm descended from men whose love language was protection, a protection so fierce it sometimes felt like terror.

     b   He was and he is not. Of Iskandar, I have no photographs. I could not find any public record of his birth in Lebanon, nor of his untimely death in Mexico. It was as if he didn't exist. He was worth less than a single footnote in the history of the Ottoman Empire.

6   But surely he must have existed, as I exist. I carry his father's name, tucked inside my last. I am given to be Lover of Horses, Earth-lover.

7   Grandpa said Iskandar could bend a dime between his thumb and forefinger. He would tie his shoe while standing up, like an ibis on one leg. He could catch a fly with his eyes closed. When he leapt, he hovered in the air like a hawk. He was as tall as the sky.

8   "On closer inspection, Grafton informs us, appearances of uniformity are deceptive. To those of us who are not experts on the footnote, they seem to be 'solid and fixed'" (Anthony Grafton, *The Footnote: A Curious History* [Les Editions du Seuil, 1997]).

14

اسكندر المقاتل الشجاع
المسلم مقيّداً.
في القرية في الأسفل، طلقات رصاص. سقط اسكندر [9]
رصاصة في ساقه. [10] [11] [12] [13]

المسلم المقيّد سحبه
سالماً خلف شجرة أرز.
اعطى اسكندر الرجل مفتاحه،

---

[9] Lebanese poet Dana Cheaib notes, "The translator uses the term قرية for 'little town.' What's the difference between a village and a little town?"

[10] *Send Agha Skandar,* it was said, after other Ottoman soldiers failed to capture the Muslim stealing the town's water. In the 1860s, clashes between Muslims and Christians led to the burning of the town, and now this man had diverted the river for his fields!

[11] *Agha,* in Turkish, is an honorific. Send Boss Skandar. The story flows down to me from my father.

[12] This is not the only bullet Skandar would suffer. Somehow, Skandar survived the shooting, though he was not the intended target. The man he captured was the target.

[13] When we were young, and my father was in a dark mood at dinner, he'd sometimes bark at our mother. I hid in quietness. If I could be silent enough. Still enough.

---

14 Bullet : body :: footnote : text? Or body : footnote :: bullet : text?

15 My father told me that Skandar was shot in the leg, but not precisely where. I imagined it was his calf. The notes at the bottom of a page are called "footnotes" because they appear as footers. Once, while playing basketball, I pulled a muscle in my calf and it felt like I was shot. I'm a weekend warrior. Sprained ankles, plantar fasciitis, bruised metatarsals, and Achilles tendonitis: each injury reminds me how much I rely on my feet, which largely are hidden from me.

16 Why did the Muslim man save Skandar's life? After all, he was a Christian, a foot soldier for the empire.

17 Nabokov once said, "I want translations with copious footnotes, footnotes reaching up like skyscrapers to the top of this or that page so as to leave only the gleam of one textual line between commentary and eternity."

18 My father, however, was also a deeply tender man. He'd always greet us with hugs, and asked for hugs in return. He'd call me "honey" in front of my teenage friends. I was so embarrassed. At night, driving me home from high school, he'd play classical music, place his arm over my shoulder, touch the back of my head. When I made him proud, he never hid his tears, even in public. I'm the age he was then, unable to hold back tears when my children shine.

19 One day in the 1980s, in the dim living room in Brooklyn, my grandfather lounged in his easy chair, and I was sitting on the couch. The Mets, his favorite team, flared on the screen. The ball hurtling and cracking against the mitt. We listened to the play-by-play, a remnant of radio days, a running footnote to the game, offering narrative description, statistics, and stories. One of the players kneeled down to tie his shoelace. *My father,* he said in the dark, *could tie his shoelace standing up.* After he lost his shirt in the 1960s in a failed business deal in Argentina, Grandpa sank into a dark depression. He'd invested all his money and then the government was overthrown, and all his contacts were lost. It was like he went underwater. His wife, Lily, would get up every day and make him his coffee, before heading off to work at the school cafeteria. The rest of the family went about their days, pretending the house wasn't sinking. He didn't get out of bed for the better part of a year.

20 Why did Skandar let him go? Why did the Ottomans not believe Skandar that he failed to catch the man? When I return to Deir al-Qamar, years later, I search the eyes of everyone I meet, looking for answers. For what it would have meant to stay.

21 But what I know of Arabic I've scraped together from curses and caresses, from the Babbel app.

22 Most people know little or nothing about their great-grandparents, and nothing at all about the generation older than that. We also disappear from human memory.

السجن أو المنفى؟ [23] [24] المنفى، [25] [26] [27]

على الأقل، حرية. لكن أين تكون الحرية؟

خلف الأسوار البعيدة

للإمبراطورية العثمانية، بيت بلا

قضبان حديدية في النوافذ،

حيث الماء يسيل من كل صنبور—

أو هكذا تقول الحكاية. [28] [29] [30] [31]

---

23   In the original poem, I left out that Iskandar's wife, my great-grandmother Elena, appealed to the jailers to let him go. She pleaded to save his life. How had I forgotten?

24   I phone my oldest relative, Great-Aunt Helen, named after her grandmother Elena (Helen). She's ninety-one. When she was a small child, she tells me, her grandmother gave her a bath, swishing the water around her with her hands. Elena died before my father was born, and because of my grandfather's silence, we never heard a word about her. I cup this single image of Elena like cool water poured into palms.

25   The jailers agreed, on one condition: he could never be seen in Lebanon again. What is hunger but the softness of palms, hidden beneath the hardness of the fist. Cue: door opening. Cue: the bustle in the house, one last time. Elena bundled my grandfather and carried him out, minding two other children as they prepared to leave the house forever.

26   What if the most important thing is concealed in the footnotes? My grandfather's hands grew soft with the years, the skin almost like silk. I remember how, in Grandfather's last years, my father would hold his father's hand, like a mother holding a child's hand.

27   According to public records, Elena died of cervical carcinoma in 1935 at the age of forty-eight. In 2022, Elena, I sit at your grave in St. John Cemetery in Queens for the first time with my cousin Jesse. Your name is carved on the left side of the stone. The right is bare. Where Skandar should have been.

28   Elena, when my daughters ask where we come from, I'll begin with mountains and a voice of light. A woman bargaining with empire. Fugitive from injustice, refuge to your brood.

29   Great-Aunt Helen had never heard the story of what caused the family's exile. It was and it was not.

30   And when it was time to descend the mountain, no one followed them.

31   كان ياما كان

Translation (Sam)

When Salomon (Sam) is born in 1910
Iskandar first appears
  —translated:

el ciudadano Alejandro Metriz

He's born
borne across the archive
citizen / father

Fleeing Salina Cruz after the Murder (Close-Up: Adell)

Eighteen, your hand promised, you leave all your forbidden longings behind: going to a movie in a theater, joining your own graduation party, kissing a boy. Everything your father kept you from. You'd shimmied out the window, lain prone on the roof to watch classmates cha-cha, cheek to cheek in the town square. Now, your father's gone in the ground. Now northbound train, a book of poems in your lap, everything you own hurtling toward El Norte, America, and marriage. If this were a movie, the camera would pan back from book to hand to train car after train car, endless track racing across endless land. Cut to Jimmy, your brother, his face blazing, breath huffing from the lug. These bags—why so heavy? he rages. He tears the book from your grasp—. Your mouth agape at him, as he tosses it out the train's open window. He reaches inside your bag, grabbing another book, and another, and another—flinging them all into—

Your eyes, now darkened
cataracts, look back, look back
& won't let go

man·i·fest (ii)

\ˈma-nə-ˌfest\

    1. a document giving comprehensive details of a ship and its cargo and other contents, passengers, and crew for the use of customs officers

As in *The manifest failed to disclose where the passengers intended to go*
upon arrival at the port

Antonym:
memory

    2. display or show (a quality or feeling) by one's acts or appearance; demonstrate

As in *Father manifested signs of severe depression*

Antonym:
withhold

    3. to record in a manifest

As in *Every passenger shall be manifested at the point*

of departure

Border Lines (Laredo Crossing, 1923)

there is a place near
where we don't belong

the place where we belong
and lose our way

this is where we need
follow it to its end

to find the bridge
of another beginning

The Arab Crosses into Los Estados Unidos

Once I bathed in new phrases,
spoke with the starthroat.

Silked in sentences, curled
inside the parentheses

of dream. Once my father bent
a dime between his index

and his thumb, snapped a house
from air, swallowed gold fire

captured in singing glass. Glass
sang from his circling touch.

But when they came for him,
he danced to their orchestra

of bullets.
                    We did not wait
to tuck him safely

into earth, raise his name
in stone.
                    What
we buried we buried

beneath our ribs.

                    At the border
of the country

of

                    the future—

I own nevers,
            dusty

keys

        with no receiver.

I carry him

                and cross the river.

I.

النسيب

Of Fate & Longing

*The whole world is a narrow bridge—the essential thing
is not to be paralyzed by fear.*

Rabbi Nachman of Bratslav

This Sea, Wrought & Tempestuous

this is the transcript

of after

saying, Arise

the boat   not

bodies

not   not the first such

find

cannot   scribe

A Map of Migration Routes

Each line is arrowed red.
Inside, they tumble
across muscled continents

like erythrocytes, millions
of flesh-tucked skulls hauling
dreams. Red for departure,

blue for return. Their lives
shrunk to a single cell
they palm to their chest

in bus depots and windowless tents
at night, seeking a signal,
a recognizable voice, someone

home, lithium ions draining.
When given paper and crayons,
their children draw weapons.

Red for departure, blue
for return. Like veins, the lines
draw back to the heart, the heart

where the rivers flooded,
the fields baked in drought,
where the guns came out—

and guns made love to guns,
making more guns,
and the blood began to run.

Disparate Impacts

The Testimony of Joseph Gaston

I've moved around
my whole life
        Cincinnati Columbus Nashville Cleveland

    after I got out
    of prison

            I was homeless for just
            over five years

                always in motion

                            "Judge Boyko . . . to take senior status." (Cleveland.com)

nobody but nobody
would rent to me

                            *"I intend to maintain
                            pretty much a full docket,
                            but maybe a little less to enable me
                            to travel and sit on other courts,"
                            Boyko said.*

        I went to ten different apartments
        their management companies
                all rejected me
        for felony conviction

                it was discrimination

I got so fed up I asked Legal Aid
I asked the Urban League
the Ohio Civil Rights Commission
but no one would

                                    represent me

everyone told me it was a useless fight
        told me the judge would rule
                        against
                everyone told me to wait

        so I took three months
        filed my own case

                based on "disparate impact"

                        it was a good
                        lawsuit really beautiful

Plaintiff contends the Defendants engaged in discriminatory housing practices, including refusal to rent, discrimination in rental terms and refusal to make reasonable accommodations in rules, policies and practices, in violation of the Fair Housing Act. He further alleges he has a disability which substantially impair[s] major life functions, but he does not elaborate on what his disability is. It appears he may be suggesting his prior conviction is a disability.

                every housing discrimination case
                        goes to Judge Boyko

                everyone knows Judge Boyko
                        Judge Boyko has performed well
                                for the system

Opinion and Order: Plaintiff's Motion to Proceed In Forma Pauperis *(Doc. No. 2) is granted, his Motion for Temporary Restraining Order and Preliminary Injunction (Doc. No. 3) and his Motion for Appointment of Counsel (Doc. No. 4) are denied, and this action is dismissed pursuant to 28 U.S.C. §1915(e). The Court certifies, pursuant to 28 U.S.C. § 1915(a)(3), that an appeal from this decision could not be taken in good faith. Judge Christopher A. Boyko on 2/27/2019.(S,SR)*

So I just
gave up

I wore out my eyes
I'm nearsighted now, need
glasses to read

what I see:
the system is rigged

"It's meaningful, it's rewarding, frustrating
at times, just like anything else," the judge said.
"But overall, I couldn't ask for a better job."

Cuyahoga County is a haven
for housing
discrimination

an incestuous marriage
between the legal system
and the homeless situation

they can't let you
win

representative democracy looks like
a good idea
but you can diminish
the role of the populace

"Division hurts, and it's felt
everywhere, I think," the judge said.

I was homeless for over
five years on a waiting list at EDEN
five
years

no one should have to wait five years for housing

some guys tried to jump me
in the shower at 2100 Lakeside
I didn't comply

they threw me out

living in the streets, sleeping
in the woods

raised enough
for a car, started
sleeping there

then in trains and buses

some drivers let you ride all night long

I liked the 22
downtown to the airport
and back

it's a long route

other drivers make you get off

it's a hard life

I wouldn't want anyone
to suffer like that

used to shower in the rec center
kept my bag with me

kept my hygiene up

but I never begged
     I wasn't brought up
       like that

At the naturalization ceremony,
Judge Boyko reads a poetic statement
by Dean Alfange:

"I do not choose to be a common man . . .
I will not trade freedom for beneficence
Nor my dignity for a handout
I will never cower before any master
Nor bend to any threat.
It is my heritage to stand erect."

police spend most their time
harassing homeless people

I got a ticket for sleeping
     for sleeping!

     I looked it up
     there is no law that says
     you can't fall asleep
     in the state of Ohio

I almost died
     got shot at on West 25th
got blood clots in my legs
     from sleeping upright on buses

it's a hard life

     social justice institutions
     have become part of the system

everyone is part
of this system

Federal judges often work hard to maintain
their judicial independence,
as the appointment is a lifetime one.

Judge Boyko will be rewarded well

I seek no earthly reward
just change

I'm in EDEN housing on Euclid
when I got out
of prison I wanted to leave
the state
they said I had to stay:

it's called "community control"
to maintain parole
they don't want the money
leaving the state

if I live righteously, on the day of judgment
I will not be wronged

the change I seek in the system
may never become reality
but I must try

someday I'd like to be a cook
or a youth advocate

and I'd like to see the world
look into
the Peace Corps

*The judge has an offer to teach U.S. law
. . . in Ukraine and Saudi Arabia, and
having more flexibility will allow for that.*

Plague Psalm 90

Loss, you have been our regent,
Refusing the refugees
                    you sent.

Truly we're boxed in an annex
Of the mansion
                    of your text.

You turn hummingbirds to dirt
And feed humans
                    to earth.

By your annotation
                    we're smashed,
Filled with the alphabet of wrath

As the annals of our days
Wash away

Remorse for Temperate Speech

For I spoke as if I knew
to you who know

how a house looks
clothed in flames

from the inside, you
sitting in the smoke

as if watching my prose
only stoke the flames

in that stagnant room
among stagnant rooms

where the powerful
talk for your people

bound in the margins
of empire's book,

who speak and speak and speak and

May you find the وادي
where water flows

into future, and greet
what has come before,

where you did not know
you knew before,

the unmapped hidden
وادي
where past
and
future
meet

pretend to listen.

Fugitive

Where do you run, unbridled and unrequited? All night,
behind the hotel wall my head presses against, elevator shafts
rush like the driven wind, glass rooms falling and lifting

like the strange breathing I heard the translator read
yesterday, in a language I did not speak, from a script
only thirty people still remember how to read, that could

die in our lifetime. As if the ink of two thousand years
could disappear overnight. He signed my book, forgetting
my name, how we'd met years ago, another city. The brigadoons

of memory: how names rise out of mist for a day, doomed
to disappear. Like M, one I came to confide in, but did not know
saw an oasis in me. In a dorm bed she sat up, her cardigan ajar,

her underbuttons undone, furtive undercurve of her breasts
I could see and not see, in my fog, as invitation, door to a home
longed for because lost. Last night, I dreamt I left that dorm

to a street I'd never seen. How could it be I never saw this street
before, I wondered, searching for the contours of the familiar
I navigate, eyes closed. I looked and looked, my heart thrashing

against the gate of my ribs, among people without tongues, until my eyes
tired of that world and descended, like a glass lift, into this one.

Curriculum Vitae

I'll keep the ululating
        to a minimum
and wave the keffiyeh

outside the stadium.
        I'll clutch a Kalashnikov
loaded with cardamom,

and speak in tongues
        you'll equate as hatred.
I'll haul out the narghileh

in the drone museum—
        if you ask to smoke me,
I'll pretend to be plaintive.

Pimp my pride. I promise
        I'm noninvasive.
In the middle of light,

I look on the night side.
        Ask me what I do,
I'll say: unoccupied.

I'll set my nation's
        whole body on fire,
simplify the fractions

of political rhyme.
        I'll skein this skin
to the highest of high wires,

refuse to become
        a man of my time.
I'll lift the veil

off this crowded lift
       in which we are silent—
as if guilty in our climb—

and offer this tongue,
       this ripped-off gift.

Fatherhood, Insomnia, Imperial Tears

This child's cry slithers its splintering need
-les into my every nerve and widens

like the final moan of a battered amp
when the show's over. To love a baby

is to restrain the urge to bury it
inside a wall, to throw it through windows—

anything to stop its invasion. No
rocking, no breast milk, no walking will stop

the infant barbarian's imperial tears.
Fatherhood. Insomnia. Fear. She wants

to burrow inside again—by voice alone,
she does. As in the tale, the prince awakens

in woods, bell-headed, the whole golden realm
fallen into someone else's tiny hands.

Homeland

If there were one, more
would come. Even inside
the tissue, between my
index and thumb, I felt its
body writhe—its abdomen
and thorax, tiny grapes.

In the toilet, the dry paper
unfolded like a white
flower. The ant, stunned,
began to crawl down the
blooming paper. Not
finding air, it stopped,
churned its legs in a fury,
twisting like a whip, rising
on its own flagellation.

Once, in unnameable pain,
I felt as if someone were
watching me, thralled,
squeezing me between
fingers.

In flame of flesh, lit with
hurt, at the bottom of an
ocean

I awaken

Zooming Mom

Your fin-quick gaze
        now swims into view, ex-convent eyes
long uncloistered:

a mother's face is a lifetime
        of faces, voluminously lined and luminous,
now distracted by this

real-time letter. Each flourish
        of your hand blurs its swish, the back-
wash of bytes.

I've spent a life emerging
        from my image of you, and now you've gone
amniotic. We were born

to each other, mother
        and first child—our heartpumps that rumba
when thrilled or exhausted,

lungs that seize in cold,
        backs we throw out, lock us in bed for days.
In a poem, I once wrote

if the sky were a voice, it would
        be yours. The years rub it to a fluted rasp,
raspier over the audio

of compressed memory.
        My daughters—reason for this spectral
reunion—crowd the screen,

invisible bits of you
        coiled in them, their binary pool
of ancestral light.

When we watch your eyes,
	we see you looking down to where we must be
looking on your screen,

a frame below the frame of us
	looking down to you. As if a picture turns out
to be a window—

though we're locked inside
	our distant homes, and the window itself
is what's raining.

Something in us
	loves this earth, this flesh, but not enough
to cease our flailing

against its faithful
	magnetic pull. Only a day's drive away, too far
to feel this close.

Today, the headline—
	"A mission to the moon with no return
in mind." We're digital

immigrants exiled
	from the taste of your breath, the hum your lungs
thrum when you're happy

to see us, the bird
	-quick movement of you in the room,
and the room in you.

The Trees in My Chest

Again, the dream: I need to leave,
yet each door I open opens

another room, another door.
The pen in open. Is this made

possible by someone whose traces
hover in the absence? The seen

in absence. I'm aching for you,
dear architect. The further back

through history we look, the more
faces fade—a room in a house

we cannot see, nor imagine ourselves
out of. December's advancing dark.

The ember in December. I can't
breathe in this room I guest,

you ghost. The inverted asthmatic
trees in my chest burn to bloom,

& must relearn each time to rise
from the ground, & to return.

The urn in return. & the rue.

This Sea, Wrought & Tempestuous

lost in the crossing

bodies

wearing

journey

and swaying   swayed

refu   refused

respon

what shall we do unto thee

what drove these

that the sea may be calm unto us?

these refu   se

e

Border/Manifest II

Name Meters Felipe — Age ___ Sex ___ 15 M 9238
Mitri
Nationality Syria — Race Syrian
Last res. Salina Cruz Oax Mex — Dest. Lawrence Mass
ADMITTED at ___ Laredo, Texas — Date ___
OCT 1 1923
Status ___
B.S.I. No. ___ (Manifest) List No. 314 Line 14
U. S. DEPARTMENT OF LABOR
IMMIGRATION SERVICE
MEXICAN BORDER DISTRICT

Whenever Someone Mentioned Laredo, My Grandfather Would Turn Away and Curse

after Machado

LAREDO, TX. (KGNS)—The U.S.-Mexico border is seeing a tragic rise in migrant deaths, especially when it comes to illegal border crossings and officials say it's not going to slow down anytime soon. [In 2022, at least] 134 migrants have died

the system's

Traveler, there is no road;
you make your own path as you walk

along the Laredo border

you make your own road

manifest

numbers

and when you look back
you see the path

failings

released by Border Patrol

you will never
travel again

From Thy Face Shall I Be Hid

Brooklyn Heights, 1948

Like a man fighting against his mirror,
two brothers circled. Fists aloft. No words.

I couldn't tell my uncle from my father.
Years before, how did they watch their father

confront the gang alone? In his own blood,
like a man crashing against a mirror

and falling in. No forgiving the other
what each himself had failed to stop. Why could

I not tell I'd seen my uncle to my father?
At Sahadi's, I thought he was my father,

ahead in line. I'm Uncle Sam, he said.
Like a man feuding against his mirror,

he bought me three meat pies. My father
gave me prunes and the belt. Uncle patted my head.

No one knew why Uncle and my father
refused to speak for years. Now I hold the picture:

homing in, no space between their leaning heads,
they aim for the heart. A man brawls his mirror:

I can't tell my father from my father.

II.

رحيل

Of Exile

I wondered at how, as I crossed the boundary of Paradise,
Well-being, my companion, stopped and turned back,
And when I reached the border of earth, the mother of thorns,
Pains and sufferings of every kind greeted me.

Saint Ephrem the Syrian, *Hymns on Paradise*

This Sea, Wrought & Tempestuous

SHARE THIS

only to continue their journey   the transcript

translated into   another   sinking

s   way   swa   y   surf

for the sea wrought, and was tempestuous

For thou hadst cast me into the deep

Until now

only a few

have met

face of the

without

Signature Strike

His fountain pen inhales the air
to let the nib open. Black milk

his left fist smudges when he signs
his name. The ink spans continents,

dives, unfurls its bloom. Say Faheem,
who will leave his left eye

in its blot. At night, his right blurs
above the white page.

No, Daddy, Leila says, shaking
her curls at my signing—arms

crossing right beneath the neck,
hands knuckle into the fist

called love. Leila means night, dark
beauty. I'm trying to inhabit

my body but my body is night
& has its own mind.

Faheem means keen. Night thoughts
slice my lids wide. O my outcast

state, the very landscape dances,
data of pulsing shifts beneath

that which we have done & cannot
see. *Even when you don't see them,*

you can hear them, you know
they are there, is what they say

about what flies above them. Black
milk. White flight. Spine wings. Blot light.

Where they are, & how they cluster,
is signature. Abdulrahman

means servant of the merciful.
Barack means blessed. From this nib

it rises like mute thunder,
Faheem's left eye, my night's

fists crossing just above her breast.

Song for Refugees

Ooze, oud. Ease hearts whose eyes sink low.
Be hourglass in the pillaged O—.
Be wells none see. Unstopped tears,
O oud, we gather in your bowl.

O ladle of ores, scoop ink here
now seeping from the foreigner,
be sighs, O oud, and cloven aches
in the dark of millions of ears.

Be gift for famished wails and wakes
to lacks and flares and tented stakes,
the lonely outer sounds of sleeves
eating wind and drowning faces.

The oud's a lovely ark that leaks
with tales and bromides we can't keep,
and miles of ghosts before their sleep.
And miles of ghosts beneath our sleep.

Ass

There are two kinds of wild ass,
the entry begins, in *The Children's
Encyclopedia.* A favorite cuss
in Arabic: *jahash.* Speaking this tongue

is a house without a number,
inheriting a key to the door
that exists only in the I remember
of elders. Cross-references help

traveling from entry to entry.
In what country, upon crossing
the threshold of a home, would I
remove my shoes, remnant of roads?

What to carry, what should I bear
as gift to the other? *Jahash,* my father
said, laughing at the donkey ears
he'd sprouted around a fool's face.

They were born with everything
we associate with civilization
in the Fertile Crescent. Braying
means "foolish speech." Illustrations

show you what other books tell you.
Full-color photographs and maps.
The Arab American translator chooses
donkey instead of jackass,

a burnished word, almost too noble.
The burn in burnished. The key in donkey,
the Don Quixote. In the Israeli novel
The Smile of the Lamb, a dead ass rots,

caught in what journalists want
to call "the crossfire," in the heart
of an occupied town, everyone
walks past, pretends it does not exist,

refusing to move it, lingering
despite the stink, despite maggots,
as if there were nothing festering
at the center of everything. See also

Dostoyevsky's horse, in Raskolnikov's
dream, whipped about the eyes,
by a coachman who, that very night,
would turn and flay his wife.

The point: to strip the abandoned car
of all causality. Like one who awoke
to morning, after a long war,
only birds and crickets left to sing.

A language that meant exactly
what crickets mean, rubbing forelegs.
When they'd invaded the city,
commandos first seized the archives

of maps and stories. In *State of Siege,*
Darwish proposed the ass for the new flag,
half comedy and half homage.
It looks like a massacred salad, tabbouli.

Asses need little water, saith the book,
can survive eating spiky grass.
I lean and loaf. I look, don't look
up. So many bitter herbs. So much lack

to grievance. So many wounds to curse,
jawbone weapons to bless. Some stubborn,
others wisely cautious. Google *ass*
and find yourself in a forest of humans

doing things to each other we don't need
to see to believe. So much can be hidden
before us, when everything seems
at our fingertips. Dear beast of burden.

The Republic of Pain

In the republic of pain, we bloom
icebags and crutches for limbs. We plod,

doze, audition for the final repose
on therapy tables. Joints lock

without keys, muscles seize, refuse
to give back. Bones crack. We lack,

loll like eyeballs under lids, reading
the electrical map of our brains.

In this state, everyone has I, I, I
lodged on the tongue, a swelling pill

none can swallow. Windows turn out
to be mirrors. Even the trees

painted on the doors are frayed nerves.
Beyond the glass wall, the healthy unfurl

limbs, mute and patient slaves. We watch
them gallop on endless black treads,

hoist dark barbells overhead—
imagining the inevitable revolt.

The New New Colossus

Fed by the brazen gift of drought's famine,
Her tongue tasting language after language

Here at our search-burned landfill of garbage,
A migrant woman scrounges for samplings

That might fill her children's insides. Scavenge,
Mother of Exiles, on your paltry stage.

You play the part of a human bandage
On a body that will not stop bleeding.

She says: "Storied landlords, open your doors
To us, the roofless. We've hidden in swarms

To escape the dread masters of horror,
The lead-teeming automatic arms

You profit from. Welcome us, the deplored.
We stand at the landing of your golden dorm."

Upon Hearing of Plans to Remove the Gazebo

a sanctuary for Tamir

An open   place to gaze   in every direction

        you smiled eyes   restless child   baby boy in man's body

from the Latin: *see I shall*   ocean in a seashell

        you were bored   had a laugh   in camouflage hat

sanctuary   from summer sun   rain or snow

        they saw you   as threat   your fun for gun

Tamir in Arabic: owner of palm trees   wealthy one

        loved cheese pizza   ranch dressing   stuffed animals

they take you down   and we watch it: they can take you down

        loved biking   video games   and could not sit still

look I understand   why your mama wanted   that place gone

        your mama's   baby boy   will always be

on video   we watch it but cannot see   you're no martyr

        beloved boy   no one can   remove your memory

66

This Sea, Wrought & Tempestuous

from   to

only to   of what

afterward   into

face

safe

identification

citizen   ship

taken

the trans   cript of what happened

floating

the village

thy holy temple

Why are there stars?

because we need   to know   even the dark   dome

hovering above   us   its   infinite   black

like our skull   seen   from the inside   like   a bowl

      of onyx filled   with cracks   flickers   of future

        shatter   is a bright   hot snow   still   arriving

ten thousand years   from now   already dead

sending   out   their final signals   seeds   time

the way   I   hope   something I say   will come back

some dark night   when you   wrestling sheets twisting thoughts

     no   dream   though I'll have been long   translated to

ash   a phrase   will effuse   behind your eyes

    without   your knowing when   it   began

    sliding down your   spine   swimming   your restless limbs—

little glimmer .   glint of warmth .   winter ember .

Solstice Prayer

In the name of the darkness,
and of the light, in the name
of the harness of winter's ice.

In the name of the other,
and of the one, in the name
of the weather, and of the bone.

In the shame of the ache
of what I can't tell,
in the name of the break

that will not heal. In the same
of the other, and of the one,
in the name of the anterior

and the darkness to come.
In the name of the middle,
in the snow of the gloom,

in the name of the straddle
between road and home.
In the reign of the cold,

in the name of the sorrow,
in the flame of the hark
beyond morrow's morrow.

In the shame at the marrow,
in the grain of the sin
that breaks up the furrow

that I fall in. In the name
of my hands that touch
the forehead that stays shut,

then touch the sternum
that stays shut, then touch
the heart that stays shut, touch

the lungs that free the air
(what can't be said—O ghost!—)
and then lay bare.

The Fields

in the net
work joints
twist & sup

port each
other
a complex

I try to find
a handle
for floating

but it slips
from me
my body

bridges
nodes
to nodes

stretches
& bends
to step

a mother
board
a dusty city

oil refinery
from above
Corpus Christi

a memory
of grass
in the green

hard drive
nest memory
wired

inside this
little city
are cities

like Troy
holds seven
beneath cities

I want to
hold close
your soft

city & yet
the angles
cut in

a map
of a metro
of a country

that's given up
name stations
after heroes

handle
attached
to handles

a shovel
I can't grasp
to break

hide
from me
this net

work ribs
holding in
sides in, in

arced art
eries interior
of becoming

civilization
& pumped
from earth

every line
a sign
of humans

a mirror
this mirror
mirrors

The Menagerie (and the Beautiful Barbed Wire)

This one has no face, and tilts her head like a sail catching wind.
And all
This one has twenty feet and they all point backward.
Of us carved
This one's elephant ears tell the caliber of fired ammunition.
By vertical
This one's eyes are eggs boiling, but not yet hard.
Bars

This one's head is a marble flickable by a child's thumb.
All of us
This one's head the size of a globe, actual size.
Wider than eyes
This one has no chin, and chews gum with her gums.
Mum
This one has a tongue that fits in the mouth when tied.
As lies

This one's words are rocks, and breath is tear gas.
Surrounded
This one has a hole in his center you can see right through.
By towers with
This one can't remember anything after the bombing passed.
Undisturbed
This one's stumps can hug you like good news.
Views

This one remembers what he's never witnessed.
We call out
This one's skin folds in, and her organs flop around.
But our mouths

This one is a ghost that has never been a guest.

> *Utter*

This one can only breathe underwater, and in air will drown.

> *No sound*

This one dreams of toasted pistachios in ice cream.

> *Walls dream*

This one dreams of her father's resurrection.

> *Or die*

This one dreams of sand beaches and learning to swim.

> *Rising*

This one wakes in prison, having dreamed all night of prison.

> *Or riven*

This Sea, Wrought & Tempestuous

to   ward

the   shores

of the silence

an   *d the*

y   *s*

h   *a*

ll

have

re aching out to

n   *o*

p   *l*   *a*   ce

o f   i   dentification

to

re   *s*   *t*   *the*   *i*

r   *he*   *a*

d

faced with

this   sea

Qasida for Abdel Wahab Yousif

***

in the dream, I wake
treading the underwater
in the black beneath I see

like horses galloping
the gloom of the sea
they wrestle the living salt

fight to rise to the shore of light
but their pockets and shoes are full
of the stones of grief

their mouths open
to no words

but stones

and why do I see them
from beneath

***

"Shipwreck off Libya"

I read the head
-line and the story
and you are
nowhere inside
you are among the forty-five
missing and presumed

***

Ya Abdel Wahad Yousif, I
                call out to you

                        at the boundary of salt and sky
                        aching for echo

I can't fit the sea in the basin

                between my ears

                    ***

                You are destined to go

you wrote, which, when it touches
our eyes and tongue, means our

                    head rocked by the roaring waves,
                    [our] body swaying in the water,
                    like a perforated boat

                                      carrying dozens of

                                          [of obscure origin]

      sea   missing and presumed

          capsizing

76

***

"From Darfur to Libya he scraped his way"

Ya Abdel, how could you see
and still climb into the boat
and not turn away

       You'll die at sea

                              the waters prevailed

       You'll die at sea

you wrote it was destiny
but isn't destiny
another name
for

              dying:
          Time. Language.
          Songs. Love. Music.

***

forgive us our imperial
din
forgive us our doorless
borders

***

قَالَ رَبِّ اغْفِرْ لِي وَهَبْ لِي مُلْكًا لَا يَنْبَغِي لِأَحَدٍ مِنْ بَعْدِي ۖ إِنَّكَ أَنْتَ الْوَهَّابُ

Lord, forgive me, and grant me
a kingdom

that no one
should follow after me

***

Ya Abdel,

I dreamed of you last night, holding
the sea in your arms like a lover, you
kissing its wet mouth, you
at last at rest in its endless bed, your heart
knocking me awake, as if
I could not

***

why should the waters prevail

***

it's all in vain

you write,

no flash of light
to scare away the darkness

***

the jaws of the sea
waving
the only welcoming

***

may God grant you a kingdom beyond
      the kingdom of empires

and warlords beyond
              the kingdom of the sea beyond

the kingdom of the drowning stones beyond

the kingdom of the kingdom
                  beyond
      the kingdom belonging to no one
because it belongs to everyone beyond
the doors of the sea

a floating place, a garden   the waters will veil

          a garden of words
          beyond words

      that rises

Border/Manifest III

Passage Manifest

NATIONAL ARCHIVES

Card Manifest Data Sheet (Early Form 548)

Additional information may be recorded on the reverse side of the card if the alien appeared a decision concerning deporting or barring him/her from entering the U.S. Also subsequent re-entry by the alien may also be noted on the reverse side.

MANIFEST		Port of: Laredo, TX	Date: October XX, 1923	Serial No.	

Family Name: (In the cellar of the) Metres (store) — **Given Name:** Adeíl (is hidden to prevent) — Accompanied by: Iskandar (holds up his hands)

He gives the bandits what they ask — Hide it in your sock, Jimmy says, this pocketknife, you will need it when—

C.I.V. No. Iskandar	Place and date of Issue gives the bandits what they ask	Section and Subdivision But they come back again	Quote Country Charged The knife is like a seed that will	flower with bandits' blood	R.P. NoP.V. No.

| Place of Birth
Whenever they come back again.
When we visit Jimmy in the city | Age
his dreams still bloom
with blood | Yrs.
Mos. | Sex
He ties
his tie
so tight. | It looks
W. D.
like a noose | Occupation
Lives in Building 13,
Co-Op City | Read
Write
to find | It's impossible |

Language or Exemptions — Nationality — Last Permanent Residence (Town, Country, etc...)
A way to make it loose — How does he undo it at night? — The bat my father keeps beneath his bed

Name and Address of Nearest Relative or Friend in Country Whence alien came
it waits to be let loose. You have to know when to grab.

Ever in U.S.? Like the bat beneath	From my father's bed	To For when the bandits come back	Where To keep your people safe	Passage Paid By

Destination and Name and Complete Address of Relative or Friend to Join There
You have to know when to grab. — he says,

Money Shown Ever Arrested and Deported or Divided from Adversaries When the bandits come back again		Purpose of Coming and Time Remaining In the center of the family store	

Head Tax Status To keep	Height his people safe	Complexion	Hair Iskandar	Eyes	Distinguishing Marks holds up his hands

Seaport and Date of Landing, and Name of Steamship — Con. Im. Identification Card

Records By	Previously Examined at	Date	Previous Deposition	Present Deposition or P.I.	Arrived by

U.S. Department of Labor, Immigration Services — Form 548

National Archives and Records Administration — NARA's website is www.archives.gov — NA Form 14132g (3/06)

American Family Photograph, circa 1929

Back then, they knew how to dress—the men in three-piece suits cut snug to the body, the women in silk and velour and heels. As if their clothes would allow them, recent arrivals in their third country, to disappear into the safety of respectability.

Sitting on the left, Elena, my great-grandmother, bears the only look that approximates a smile. I mistook her for her daughter Adell, missing from the photo. She's pinned a flower above her right breast. Her pleated skirt shines. Her beauty is not her daughter-in-law Teresa's wide-set eyes, soft brows, pomaded hair clipped with barrettes. Elena's look, a secret smile, is cool water poured into palms.

Little Alexander in suit and culottes leans on his aunt Teresa—she must have doted on him. Fatherless boy named after his father. He was dead by seventeen. My father kept the funeral bill his father kept, a last memory of his little brother, planted in a foreign land before he became a man.

On the left: Naguib in Lebanon, Miguel in Mexico, and now Jimmy in New York—as if each new country requires a new identity. He's gripping the back of his mother's chair, elbows out, hands protecting his privates. His tie's knotted like a goose pecking at his neck. In his partly lidded eyes, his pursed lips, there's something coiled to the point of self-strangling, like water boiling in a teapot with no spout. His only child, with Teresa, will die at birth. He will be poured into earth.

On the right, Solomon, called Sam. Sam's tailored suit flares at the hips, feminine. His handkerchief flails from his suit pocket like a white flower. A captured bird. His ears protrude as if listening hard. He pummels his brother for fun. His eyebrows stitch elegant over his nose. He'll throw a man from a train for flirting with his cousin. He'll earn his life designing dresses. See his hands like birds winging a pattern in the air.

In the middle, Philip, my grandfather, stands, his oiled black hair parted so sharp it looks carved by a knife. His shirt so white it glows, a ghost. Into his seventies, he wore a three-piece suit, his arthritic fingers fumbling over buttons to cover his chest. In the photo, his hands are hidden.

I want to see again his hands that turned to silk when he reached the end. The same hands that thrashed his sons into terror and flight. Hands that gripped cue sticks and cigarettes. He was so young then.

What I have are his eyes. Look: the softness there.

Beneath ferocity's shield, a child's gaze shadowed by fear.

That everyone looks past the camera, off to their left, as if someone has just entered the room.

Look:

Tweets to Iskandar from the Capital, One Hundred Years after His Death

1.

Great-Grandfather,
I wish you could see
this land your children's
children now wander—

how from three directions
you can't even perceive
the palace of the emperor
for the leaf-lush trees.

2.

The dredged reflecting pool
looks roughly like the flesh
beneath my ruptured nail.
The stone tower unleashes

and roots down its double.
If you could see my face,
would you see your face
hovering back like a skull?

3.

This is the stone and water
for the millions who died
fighting in a war called good.
Your son warred a war

before and after the war
against everyone who didn't die.
For my empire, should I
object or volunteer?

4.

The war no one won
almost drowned
my father your grandson
in its black stone.

He carries the stone
hidden in his spine—
and all the names
he couldn't save.

5.

When they came for you
and brandished their guns
in your store in Salina Cruz—
you could not imagine

El Norte any more
than I imagine I hear
you plead in two tongues
to spare your children.

6.

Are you the secret reason
my father's at home
speaking any tongue
of all the migrant people

he welcomes as kin?
He holds the umbilical
passage to the homeland
beneath his olive skin.

7.

In the heart of empire
I swallow my sword
and exhale a great fire,
hollow out my words

until they can float
you over the stolen river.
My heart and its borders
swarm with migrant hope.

III.

فخر

Of Return

O grace abounding and allowing me to dare
  to fix my gaze on the Eternal Light,
  so deep my vision was consumed in it!

I saw how it contains within its depths
  all things bound in a single book by love
  of which creation is the scattered leaves:

how substance, accident, and their relation
  were fused in such a way that what I now
  describe is but a glimmer of that Light.

from Dante Alighieri's *Paradise* 33

The Refugee Considers the Faucet

O arm that spurts flowers,
Branch giving birth to water.
O tree that bows down

And stays there, hovering
Between sky and ground.
You anchor us to now.

We have walked so long
Our home has narrowed
To the width of our shoes

And what we can carry.
And yet you, still animal,
Hollow metal

Conducting an internal
Convo with movement,
You are endurance

In the still moment
Of beginning, you are
Anticipatory beauty,

O instantaneous river,
Compressed creek,
O brass wellspring,

Invisible lake, O slake,
Oasis in a tube, taproot,
Song of the mute, I bow

To you, and hold my hands
Like a shallow bowl
Beneath your mouth.

The Beggars of Beirut

cup their tender palms
to catch an eye, a drop

of compassion, a grain
of guilt itching inside

our shell. This one scrolls
through the dumpster

like a daily digital feed,
translating trash to dinner.

That aged one adjusts
her hijab, collapsed

in the shadow beneath
a highrise, each window

naked of glass. She
doles out packages

of napkins, searching
my face for need.

This boy sells gum—no,
a pleading smile, the gum

the key to the house
of mercy. That one sells stubs

to a ballet that once featured
her lissome legs. Today

she prays aloud to us,
imperturbable gods

with the leisure
to ignore the cries.

My lost sisters, my dear
sons, my done uncles

and drained mothers, my
beloved broken

fingers, you tap me
to the spine, column

climbing my clouded
sight, and past, rising

to a place so high
and so far, we can't be told

or held apart.

Night, Come Tenderly, Hold Us

soft in your jaws, across
your bed of wide molars.

keep your canines
at bay. night, come

tenderly, as we prepare
in pale evening, unable

to stay. restive fugitives
of day, we shelter

in swelter, in shade. trees
don't lie. inked in, we—

lashed by sudden
branches scribbling blank

on our cheeks—cross creeks
under the cold cover

toward our arcing star north.
night, we're nowhere

close & almost there.
nearing & centuries.

so we can rise,
reach the shore—

night, come tenderly.

The House at Long Lake

How a house is a self
        & else, a seeping into
of light deciding the day.
        A house so close

it breathes as the lake
        breathes. How a lake
is a shelf, an eye,
        a species of seeing,

burbling of tongues
        completing the shore.
How a loon is a probing,
        a genus of dreams,

encyclopedia of summer.
        Unsummable house
by the lake, generous hinge
        opening us. I loved,

in folds of sleep, to hear
        the back door's yawn
& click. You gliding
        down toward shore

& dawn, beyond all frames,
        reconciling yourself to
bracing Long Lake.
        Into its ever-opening, you—

Map the Not Answer

exists everything here
belonging except

desire you means
have you what for

owned never
dreams in except

وهنا تفهم للمرة الثانيه
ما هو الوطن؟

past future a
jasmine of scent

understand you here
homeland is what again

possibility in hiding
grounds reading

holds life what for
mean that lines black

out or in are you
stories in locked

you write to want that
keys find to want you

give to forgot elders
days ask you

or love make you do
you make loves do

disappearances consume you
heaven to all offer

For Leila Means Night and Night Is Beautiful to the Desert Mind

But the ends of the earth
writhe in crazy fire, so I narrow
my eyes to count each strand
upon your sweet and tender head,

replenished by their number.
Midway in this thicket, a father
now, my own skull bared
by time's flames, today I learn

for the first time the inside
of a girl's hair, to brush the hair
beneath the hair. The generous
scalp might give them up to brush,

the brush might give them up to trash,
but I will hoard their beautiful night.

Fractured (Like Chandeliers)

behind my light-olive eyes my gone grandmothers hover

and spread the old secret of the infinite regress of lovers

from others urging with others mothers merging with fathers

complete me repeatedly repeat you completely

amalgam of sojourners and crossroads of caravan

whose only roots thread from braincase to column

residing in blood the I is the join where ancestors tent

reciting repeat me completely completely repeat me

in my high laughter my gone grandfathers laugh high

a flick of a blade and your swallowed songs rise

from fluting of bone to the star map of sleepdream

O crucible of continents shifting table of contents

O cumulative quake O unfolding quote O hip bowl

you tilt as you spill into hope

Raise Your Glass

A toast to the thirst
that won't be quenched

To the drought
that dries up in the rain

A toast to the drunk
who finally stops drinking

& drinks
loneliness again

A toast to the fire
that guts the past

& clears way for future
A toast to the country

that misplaces its border guards
To the borderland

between our lives
& the dream of our lives

To the one who won the election
for a country that no longer exists

To the president
who dreams he's lost his arms

& wakes with an itchy scalp
A toast to the walls

that grow doors overnight
A toast to the migrants

the authors of movement
who write with their feet

To beauty that has no reason
but herself, a toast

A toast to the youth
who don't know

history tells them
it's not possible

To us in the middle
of the thicket

& the only way forward
is farther in

To the aged
who live their last years

where they've always lived—
in another country

A toast to the dream
of the other country

the other country that is
& is not in this one

A toast to social media
& its endless feeds

where the phone eats first
A toast to the internet

that helps us forget
what we never knew

we needed to know
To the freedom where no one is free

unless everyone is free
To the last page of the internet

which reads:
GO THE FUCK OUTSIDE

A toast to the host & the guest
the ghost & this house

where we die together tonight
& rise in some distant yesterday

our bodies hiding in the light
of a forgotten open page

Learning the Ancestors' Tongues

you want to learn I
more me knowing

                  place one in accord with all were they

know I than
myself

            sound a came there suddenly and
            wind mighty rushing of as heaven from

language this
me inside

            sitting were they where house the all filled it and

flames in ancestors dear

                    fire of as like tongues cloven
                    them of each upon sat it and

now me with are you

                  tongues other with speak to began

delight in me watching
                you feeling

            holy the with filled

me through

            tongues other

heard man every
language own his in speak them

backward looking I'm

        God of works wonderful the tongues our in speak them hear do we

wipers like reading

        speak them

erase to not trying write

        hear

flames in ancestors dear

        we do

consumed not but burning

do we   *we do*

كما في السماء كذلك على الارض

consumed but not burning

we do   *hear we*

view the clear

        tongues

hovering hovering

next is where to

Never Describe the Sky as Azure

unless it's made of stone.
        لاجورد Lāzhward

migrating from Persia,
        smuggled from Farsi

to Arabic, & thrown
        like a wingless bird

across the sky-dark sea
        until its version

spills from English mouths.
        Lapis lazuli.

O trap of beauty,
        you are a fiction . . .

Exhausted, at day's end
        of an oven-summer

I duck out of the house
        into the truth of twilight

blue. No other name
        than azure, azure,

and no other home
        the color of this sky

struck above this earth,
        no path to heaven

except through this dirt.

Entre Naranjos

Dear unrhymable, you repel
my word-hoard, unharnessable

wild horse pausing beneath
the last wild apple in the last

unincorporated field
in the world. In you, Sanskrit

gardens hang. In German,
you hail from China. Persian

emperors kneel before you.
In Russian, I recall you as apple

seen. To unpeel you
from you is to be stung sudden

by sweetness. I've longed
so long for you, unrhymed, I live

in two time zones. The before
is now our after, long past

our laughter, the tower of tears.
We've been so long together

it was like we were apart. Now
it's time to wend and wind back

to the field, the tent and want
of the wind. Let me lie down

in you, unsplit, as you
devour my mouth.

The House of Refuge

The Testimony of Chaplain Christana Gamble

On a hot June morning during the pandemic, we Zoomed into each other's separate Cleveland rooms. Her virtual background: space, a sky of stars, and a dark planet rimmed by light. Mine: an office, shelves lined with books . . .

I love the library

You know I'm pretty
                much an open book
and I want to share my story
         because it helps others

a violet flower
tucked in her
pulled-up hair

(Be with us, Lord,
        as I enter
          my story):

I was born in Hickman Mills, Missouri,
to a white preacher and a Black mother
in the sixties

Before Cleveland, I was in the country
           riding on horses
       not living in public
        housing

When they divorced, I moved
from a white world
       to Cleveland, Mom's breakdown

shock treatment

in foster care
(God blessed me quick
        but I was rebellious)

at Metzenbaum Children's Center
and public housing, I knew
        something was not right

it wasn't clean
it was wild

and I adapted to the atmosphere

My boyfriend was a dealer
        and I let him in my house
I was nineteen

The first time I went to court,
        they kept saying

                                                trafficking,
                                                trafficking

and I didn't know
        what they were talking about

I was nineteen
and Judge Gaul didn't ask me if I needed
        treatment:

                                        what's more
                                        important
                                                the drugs
                                        or your child?

When I came home, I don't know
        how I ended up
in the same . . .

more drugs, prison
                again

        Why? You go through the programs
                and probation
                        you work
                the case plan
        and you still have no housing

and never knew it was illegal
        until last year, you see
                the system was not made for me

the indigo
screen dances
around her
like a dreamcoat

        But God, His hand, His
                        hand

Everything that has happened has led
to this

(God, I cannot leave Him off my lips)

I've been in and out of County all my life

I've been in City Mission I've been in Women
in Transition I've been in CATS
I've been in prison I've been in foster care
I've been homeless I've lived under bridges

I've been through all of that
                    and so I know

Ever since I was little, my mom
            always asked why
                    I brought in the strays

Don't they have a home? she'd say

            But that's how I've been

Because if you don't have a safe place to dwell
the afflictions
will descend

I looked and looked
I waited and waited
                            EDEN shelter care
finally
took me in   mental illness diagnosis
                    unwrote my record

Northeast Ohio Coalition for the Homeless has been
my tent

and now I've made the House of Refuge

her phone rang,   (a client)
she said,
and answered it

Chaplain Gamble
may I help you

and all went mute
for a moment, indigo

background
dancing on her skin

her words for her
client alone

          I'm back

she said

          and so my heart

          My ministry, the House of Refuge
               a peaceful restful
                     place

          The House of Refuge is up and ready
               the fridge
          is full
                     the microwave is ready

          because of my past I was always afraid

          I'm untaught but I'm trained by the Lord

          What I want for people
               is what God gave me

          food, atmosphere, a people that love you
          without feeling
                   degraded

          and so my heart and I am so glad to say that I can
               confidently
               and passionately

          all along I've been trained

I was walking down the street and the Lord
        spoke to me
               and said, open the door

And I'm not afraid of my past anymore

And the door opened

You Have Come Upon People Who Are like Family and This Open Space

know cannot I
end will this how
both are we though

air different in breathing
flesh different of planets
stop won't I

hand my holding
you toward
اهلا وسهلا

people upon come have you
family like are who
space open this

space this open
you welcome I that
away turn to

stay to wish you unless
shoes your remove and rest
speak your into lean we

slake to drink tender
eat to fullness and
end the are you

beginning my of
of beginning the
end my

Devotional

Light my face and light the flesh of my flesh,
Light each my eyes and light inside my sight,
Light the light that makes me light in the bones,
And in my hands, light, and in my loins, light,

And light your light before and behind me,
Above and beneath me, light to my right
And light to left, light to my enemies
Who in the moral dark will use my light

Against me, light the dull swords of my ribs,
The thick fist within, light the blood-hot rooms
Pulsing there, light the gates when they swing wide
To the stranger, light more light on my tongue,

In the light, light more light, in the black, light,
And when it's time to snuff this wick—light that light.

Afterword

The mass human migrations due to the Syrian civil war, Trump's Muslim ban in 2017, the ongoing crisis along the southern border of the United States, and the war on Ukraine—over the past decade, I've found myself poring over news story after news story, reading with a particular fury, angered by the indifference of those in power who use borders to divide us and use the other as political fodder.

Refugees come from every continent and background. The United Nations High Commissioner for Refugees reports that at the end of 2022, over 108 million people have been forcibly displaced from their homes, and over 35 million of them are refugees. Syria, Ukraine, and Afghanistan accounted for 51 percent of the refugees in the world. The scope of the problem is dizzying.

These images and stories of people caught in the fire zones of global violence bothered me the way they would bother anyone. But they also triggered one of my earliest memories. When I was five, in the blazing heat of Camp Pendleton outside San Diego, I walked past row after row of burlap tents, the dust stinging my eyes and tickling my nose. Until we were there, meeting the Vietnamese family my parents had promised to sponsor. *But where is their home?* I asked my mother. I couldn't imagine what it was like to lose a home. They lost not only a home, of course, but also a whole country. A country they would never return to. Yet my parents helped them find a place to live. We'd visit their new home and they'd receive us like family. We are still family.

It wasn't until I started writing these poems and drawing together family history that it came to me how much these stories of refugees that I have known or read about rhymed with our own family stories of migration, particularly the one passed down from my grandfather and father (both also named Philip).

We never used the term *refugee,* but my grandfather was a refugee, who fled Lebanon after his father, my great-grandfather, Iskandar ibn Mitri Abourjaili, was exiled for disobeying the Ottoman army. It's a story I tried to tell in "The Ballad of Skandar," published in *To See the Earth,* and explore in another way here.

This is what I know: after leaving Lebanon, the family wound up in the growing port city of Salina Cruz, Mexico, around 1908. It was a time of civil unrest, but that didn't stop Iskandar, known locally as Alejandro, from establishing a dry goods store. However, in 1923, Iskandar was robbed twice. The first time, he bought off the bandits. The second time, he was murdered, causing the family to flee their home once again, this time north into the United States.

In 2020, I'd hoped to travel to Salina Cruz to find the grave of my great-grandfather, but COVID hit, and I had to do research from home. On Facebook, I triangulated with a local woman, Myrna Ramirez. She went to the Panteón Municipal cemetery, and wrote back: "The municipal manager of the pantheon tells me that there are only 4 foreigners buried. The graves that are not claimed in a certain time are ceded to other people." In all likelihood, I would never find his grave. I was heartbroken.

But once I wrote the poems of "Border/Manifest," and sat and prayed with them, something in me changed.

Many of the poems in this book are a conversation with Iskandar, an attempt to make peace with all he and his family endured—and what they could not endure. I didn't need to find his grave in Mexico. He is with me, part of me. That is why I am here.

Iskandar, I know you are with me every day, watching over me, and I thank you. To all my ancestors, thank you. May you rest.

شكراً لكم أيها الأجداد

To those who came before, to those who find themselves here, and those who will come, may these poems give you refuge.

Notes

"قَصِيدَة"

See https://en.wiktionary.org/wiki/قَصِيدَة#Arabic for more about this word.

"Qasida for the End of Time"
Inspired by the ancient Arabic form and its tripartite structure, and innovative recent iterations by Khaled Mattawa, in particular. The plague psalms in the book work with the Hebrew psalms.

"Border/Manifest"
For the ancestors, particularly Iskandar and Elena. Also great gratitude to Helen Nahom, whose long memory put some pieces of the family puzzle together for me. Thanks as well to my father, for his passion for family.

"The Arab Crosses into Los Estados Unidos"
A poem in my grandfather's voice, based on what he told me and what he could not tell me.

"This Sea, Wrought & Tempestuous"
For all those lost in the crossings. The original text was an urgent email sent in 2014, calling on activists to place pressure on governments to rescue migrants at risk of drowning in the Mediterranean. A decade later, the same problems continue.

"Disparate Impacts"
Special thanks to Joseph Gaston for sharing his story. Thanks as well to Maria Smith of the Legal Aid Society of Cleveland for connecting us. You can find online versions of "The House of Refuge" and this poem with footnotes, which explore the problem of routine housing discrimination for those with criminal records: https://www.thebeliever.net/logger/never-ending-sentences/. In 2015, the US Supreme Court ruled that the Fair Housing Act included disparate impact claims, which now makes it against the law to exclude an applicant simply on the basis of having a criminal record. However, landlords too often continue to ignore the law.

"Remorse for Temperate Speech"
After W.B. Yeats. For two Palestinians, Raghad Salah and Mosab Abu Toha, who on separate occasions bore my intemperate temperance gracefully.

"Whenever Someone Mentioned Laredo, My Grandfather Would Turn Away and Curse"
This poem uses lines from Antonio Machado's untitled Caminante poem, translated by Mary G. Berg and Dennis Maloney.

"From Thy Face Shall I Be Hid"
For my father, Philip Metres Jr., based on his story.

Saint Ephrem the Syrian's hymn on paradise was translated by Sebastian Brock.

"Signature Strike"
According to the Bureau of Investigative Journalism, a "signature strike" is the term used for a drone strike "where the identity of the person/persons targeted is not known but their 'pattern of life' or behavior indicates they are involved in terrorist activity." Signature strikes emerged into public awareness in 2008 and thereafter gained notoriety under Barack Obama.

"Song for Refugees"
Thanks to Robert Frost, by way of Omar Khayyam. For oud player Mohamad Zatari, one of millions who fled Syria during the civil war that began in 2011.

"The New New Colossus"
With apologies to Emma Lazarus.

"Upon Hearing of Plans to Remove the Gazebo"
This poem is for Samaria Rice, in memory of her son Tamir, murdered by Cleveland police in 2014 for waving a toy gun. He was twelve.

"*Why are there stars?*"
A poem in response to my daughter Leila's question.

"The Fields"
For Etel Adnan, after her painting *Oil Fields*.

"Qasida for Abdel Wahab Yousif"
In memory of Abdel Wahab Yousif, a Sudanese poet also known as Latinos, who in a poem predicted his own death in the Mediterranean Sea, in August 2020, as he sought refuge in Europe.

The quote from *Paradise* was translated by Mark Musa.

"The Refugee Considers the Faucet"
After Pamela Argentieri's sculpture *Continued Persistence*.

"Night, Come Tenderly, Hold Us"
For Dawoud Bey, after his photograph *Untitled #19 (Creek and Trees),* from the series *Night Coming Tenderly, Black*.

"The House at Long Lake"
For Amy Breau, and the Breau family.

"Map the Not Answer"
An Arabic simultaneity for Marwa Helal. It quotes Mahmoud Darwish, from *Journal of an Ordinary Grief.* And here you understand, for a second time, what is home.

"Fractured (Like Chandeliers)"
For the ancestors.

"Raise Your Glass"
This poem is after Fadhil al-Azzawi's "Toasts," translated by Khaled Mattawa, whose performance with al-Azzawi in 2008 also inspired "A Toast (for Nawal Nasrallah)."

"Learning the Ancestors' Tongues"
An Arabic simultaneity, meant to be read in two voices, one right to left, and the other left to right, overlapping or meeting at the center.

"The House of Refuge"
Special thanks to Chaplain Christana Gamble for her conversation, warmth, and testimony, and to Chris Knestrick of Northeast Ohio Coalition for the Homeless. Christana wants to thank Sister Linda Catanzaro for her mentorship in the Ignatian Spirituality Project while Christana was in county jail, and director Sherri Horton-Brandon for her program Women in Transition (Front Steps), which provided shelter and training for Christana as she transitioned from homelessness. To contact the House of Refuge emergency hotline for services, call 216-713-8364. To contribute to the House of Refuge, you can send a check to House of Refuge Inc., PO Box 17327, Cleveland, OH 44117. See also my note for "Disparate Impacts."

"You Have Come Upon People Who Are like Family and This Open Space"
An Arabic simultaneity, meant to be read in two voices, one right to left, and the other left to right, overlapping or meeting at the center. See also this book's welcome.

"Devotional"
Over a decade ago, I went through a dark period in which my body was racked with pain. Nothing seemed to calm my nerves. I cast about for prayers, for words that might come to balm my suffering. I tried writing my own prayers, finding the ones received from my religious education to be like locked doors, rooms without windows. This poem riffs on the Du'a of Light, a Muslim prayer, part of the Hadith. In it are echoes of the Hebrew Psalms, the St. Patrick prayer, Quaker prayers ("holding you in the Light"), the Kabbalah, pagan prayers to the sun, and Arseny Tarkovsky's candle in *I Burned at the Feast*.

List of Illustrations

From the Metres family archive

About the Author

Philip Metres is the author of eleven books, including *Shrapnel Maps* (Copper Canyon Press, 2020). His other works of poetry, translation, and criticism include *Ochre & Rust: New Selected Poems of Sergey Gandlevsky* (2023), *The Sound of Listening: Poetry as Refuge and Resistance* (2018), and *Sand Opera* (2015). His work has garnered fellowships from the Lannan Foundation, the National Endowment for the Arts, and the John Simon Guggenheim Memorial Foundation, as well as seven Ohio Arts Council grants, the Hunt Prize, the Adrienne Rich Award, three Arab American Book Awards, the Watson Fellowship, the Lyric Poetry Award, the Alice James Award, the Creative Workforce Fellowship, and the Cleveland Arts Prize. He is professor of English and director of the Peace, Justice, and Human Rights program at John Carroll University, and he is part of the core faculty of the MFA in Writing program at Vermont College of Fine Arts.

Poetry is vital to language and living. Since 1972, Copper Canyon Press has published extraordinary poetry from around the world to engage the imaginations and intellects of readers, writers, booksellers, librarians, teachers, students, and donors.

WE ARE GRATEFUL FOR THE MAJOR SUPPORT PROVIDED BY:

academy of american poets

OFFICE OF ARTS & CULTURE

SEATTLE

amazon literary partnership

THE PAUL G. ALLEN FAMILY FOUNDATION

CULTURE

POETRY FOUNDATION

Hawthornden Foundation

the point
envision·enact·evolve

INGRAM CONTENT GROUP

Lannan

WASHINGTON STATE ARTS COMMISSION

ART WORKS.
National Endowment for the Arts
arts.gov

The Witter Bynner Foundation for Poetry

TO LEARN MORE ABOUT UNDERWRITING
COPPER CANYON PRESS TITLES,
PLEASE CALL 360-385-4925 EXT. 103

WE ARE GRATEFUL FOR THE MAJOR SUPPORT PROVIDED BY:

Anonymous

Richard Andrews and
   Colleen Chartier

Jill Baker and Jeffrey Bishop

Anne and Geoffrey Barker

Donna Bellew

Will Blythe

John Branch

Diana Broze

John R. Cahill

Sarah Cavanaugh

Keith Cowan and Linda Walsh

Stephanie Ellis-Smith and
   Douglas Smith

Mimi Gardner Gates

Gull Industries Inc.
   on behalf of William True

Carolyn and Robert Hedin

David and Jane Hibbard

Bruce S. Kahn

Phil Kovacevich and Eric Wechsler

Maureen Lee and Mark Busto

Ellie Mathews and Carl Youngmann
   as The North Press

Larry Mawby and Lois Bahle

Petunia Charitable Fund and
   adviser Elizabeth Hebert

Suzanne Rapp and Mark Hamilton

Adam and Lynn Rauch

Emily and Dan Raymond

Joseph C. Roberts

Cynthia Sears

Kim and Jeff Seely

Tree Swenson

Barbara and Charles Wright

In honor of C.D. Wright,
   from Forrest Gander

Caleb Young as C. Young Creative

The dedicated interns and faithful
   volunteers of Copper Canyon Press

The pressmark for Copper Canyon Press
suggests entrance, connection, and interaction
while holding at its center
an attentive, dynamic space for poetry.

This book is set in Garamond Premier Pro.
Book design by Phil Kovacevich.
Printed on archival-quality paper.